The Colony of Virginia

Brooke Coleman

The Rosen Publishing Group's
PowerKids Press™
New York

To Both My Daniels

Published in 2000 by The Rosen Publishing Group, Inc.
29 East 21st Street, New York, NY 10010

Copyright © 2000 by The Rosen Publishing Group, Inc.

Photo Credits: pp. 1, 7, 11, 12 CORBIS-Bettmann; pp. 4, 8, 15, 16, 19, 20 © The Bridgeman Art Library.

First Edition

Book Design: Andrea Levy

Coleman, Brooke.
    The Colony of Virginia / by Brooke Coleman.
        p.   cm. — (The Library of the thirteen colonies and the lost colony series)
    Includes index.
    Summary: Introduces important people and events from the early years of the Virginia colony.
    ISBN 0-8239-5484-6
    1. Virginia—History—Colonial period, ca. 1600–1775—Juvenile literature. [1. Virginia—History—Colonial period, ca. 1600–1775.] I. Title. II. Series.
    F229.C67 1999
    975.5'02—dc21
                                     98-32365
                                        CIP
                                        AC

Manufactured in the United States of America

Contents

Land Ho!

Just before dawn on April 26, 1607, three ships sailed out of a terrible storm. The passengers must have cheered as they sailed into the early light of sunrise over the New

World. Of the 144 men who had boarded those ships in England, only 100 survived the four-month journey across the Atlantic Ocean. They were **colonists**. A group of **investors** called The Virginia Company had paid for their journey. They thought the colonists would discover gold in America and make them rich. Instead these men formed a **colony** that would help to make our nation.

◀ *This is a map showing what people thought Virginia looked like in 1622.*

Jamestown

The colonists steered their ships into the mouth of a deep river they named after their King, James I. As they explored the river, they were thrilled to see beautiful forests and meadows after their many months at sea. Soon they came upon an island in the river where the water was so deep that they could tie their ships right to the trees on shore. The colonists decided to settle here. They called their new town Jamestown. They built a fort out of logs from nearby trees. The walls surrounding the tiny settlement formed a triangle to protect the colonists from attacks by nearby Indians.

This modern-day copy of the ship, Susan Constant, can be seen today in Jamestown, Virginia. ▶

NEW ENGLAND

The most remarqueable parts thus named
by the high and mighty Prince CHARLES,
nowe King of great Britaine

THE PORTRAICTUER OF CAPTAYNE IOHN SMITH ADMIRALL OF NEW ENGLAND.

Ætat 37 A° 1616

These are the Lines that shew thy Face; but those
That shew thy Grace and Glory, brighter bee
Thy Faire-Discoueries and Fowle-Overthrowes
Of Salvages, much Civillizd by thee
Best shew thy Spirit; and to it Glory Wyn;
So, thou art Brasse without, but Golde within.

If so, in Brasse, (two soft smiths Acts to beare)
I fix thy Fame, to make Brasse Steele out weare.
Thine as thou art Virtues.
John Dauies. Heref:

HONI SOIT QVI MAL Y PENSE

COGNITA MIE
TENS IN SERVIT

A Scale of Leagues

Observed and described by Captayn Iohn Smith.

He that desires to know more of the estate of new
England let him read a new Book of the prospect
of new England whether he shall haue Satisfaction

1614

Simon Passeus sculpsit

Gunnells Ilz
Mr

Norwich
P. Traverse
Pembrocks Bay

P. Wigwam
Gerrarts Ils
Hoghton. Ilz
Willowby Ilz
Barty Ils

Edenborough
Cambridg
The Base
S. Iohn Towne
Leth
Peynes Pa

Schooters hill
Sandwich
Dartmouth

The River forth
Cape ELIZABTH
Harington Bay

Ipswich
P. Kent
P. Becon

Snadoun hill

Boston
Hull
Poynt Dr
Smith Iles

SouthHampton

Bristow
Salem
Fawmouth
Sangus
Charles Towne
The River CHARLES
New
Charlton
Clairborns Ils
P. Saltonstall
London
Oxford
Poynt Suttliff
Poynt George
P. Standish
NEW Plimouth
Princes Ile

Baston Ilz
Cape ANNA
Talbotts Bay

Cape IAMES
Milford hauen
STUARDS Bay
Barwick

John Smith: Adventurer and Peacemaker

The English farmboy who had dreamed of adventure while reading the legends of King Arthur and his knights became the first leader of the Virginia colony. John Smith had spent much of the sea voyage in chains below deck because he argued with the captain of the ship. Many colonists did not trust John Smith because he seemed like a troublemaker at first. They quickly changed their minds when he took on a big role in **establishing** the colony. John Smith's experience as a soldier and his common sense were essential to Jamestown's early survival. He made peace with the local Indians and gained protection from Powhatan, the most powerful chief of the local Algonquian tribe. The colonists soon followed John Smith's leadership in all their decisions.

◀ *Virginia's first leader, John Smith, is shown at the top of this map of early New England.*

Incredible Hardships

Despite John Smith's efforts to build houses and trade with the Indians for food, times were difficult for the colonists. These gentlemen knew nothing about growing crops. They planted wheat, but it wouldn't grow in the marshy, salty land. They were not ready for Virginia's hot summer, which brought many disease-causing mosquitoes to their settlement. With over half the men dead from starvation, Indian attack, or illness, Jamestown had almost become a ghost town. The 40 or so colonists left were barely alive themselves. They had just decided to return to England when a ship of 120 more colonists arrived with food and supplies.

One of the ways that John Smith kept the colonists from starving to death was by trading with the Indians. ▶

The Tobacco Boom

In 1612, things started looking up for Virginia. No one had found gold, but John Rolfe, a colonist who had arrived in Jamestown in 1610, struck another kind of gold. He followed the new English craze of smoking tobacco from a pipe. He missed his tobacco, which was very expensive in England, so he started to grow a different type of tobacco. Rolfe learned about this new tobacco from the local Indians. Soon, many colonists began growing tobacco to sell to England. By 1628, Virginia was **exporting** 500 thousand pounds of tobacco a year.

Many historians think that John Rolfe married Pocahontas, a daughter of the Algonquian chief Powhatan. Their marriage helped bring peace (for a time) between the colonists and their Native American neighbors.

◀ *Selling tobacco to people in England helped make many Virginia colonists rich.*

A Turning Point for Virginia

The year 1619 was an important one for the new colony. The first of many ships carrying women who wanted to be wives for the colonists arrived. This "bride ship" had 90 brave and eager young women aboard. Virginia's population had grown with the wealth that selling tobacco brought the colony. The first **representative** government in the New World was elected to help the Royal **Governor**, who was chosen by the English King. Men who owned land voted for two representatives, called **burgesses**, from each of the 11 counties. The House of Burgesses met in Jamestown, the capital of the Virginia colony.

Jamestown was Virginia's first capital. Later, the capital was moved to Williamsburg. The colonists hoped Williamsburg would be a great city like London or Paris.

A "bride ship" brought the first women to Virginia in 1619. ▶

Slavery in Virginia

In 1619, a Dutch ship brought the first blacks to Virginia. The huge tobacco **plantations** needed many workers, so the colonists brought Africans to America to harvest tobacco. At first they worked alongside English men and women as **indentured servants**. Like the British indentured servants, they were free to own land after they had served the time they owed their masters. After 1649, blacks could no longer own land. For the next 175 years, Africans were brought to Virginia under **brutal** conditions to work the tobacco plantations as slaves.

◀ *African slaves did the hardest work on the plantations, but they were not paid.*

The Cradle of Democracy

Some of the leaders of the Virginia Colony began to have **revolutionary** ideas about freedom. Thomas Jefferson was one man who believed that the people should govern themselves and not be ruled by a king or queen. Another Virginian, Patrick Henry, believed that the colonists should not pay taxes to England since England did not give colonists the same rights as people in England had. Their ideas were part of the strong feelings that led the American colonies to **rebel** against their English rulers in the Revolutionary War. This war for independence lasted from 1775 to 1783.

The Revolutionary War was fought to protect the rights of American citizens, but its leaders did not count black slaves or women as citizens. It would take another war, the Civil War, to gain freedom for blacks. Women had to wait until the twentieth century to gain the same rights as men.

Thomas Jefferson believed that all humans have natural rights like the right to be free and the right to govern themselves. Strangely, Jefferson, who believed in freedom, owned slaves. ▶

A Colony Becomes a State

Virginians Patrick Henry and Thomas Jefferson, along with two future United States Presidents, George Washington and Benjamin Harrison, were very important leaders of America's push for **independence** from England. Their experience in the House of Burgesses gave them the confidence that all the colonies could govern themselves as a nation. They worked with leaders from the other colonies to achieve this goal. Thomas Jefferson put their plans into words when he wrote the **Declaration of Independence**. It **united** Virginia with all the other colonies in an effort to become a nation of united states.

Patrick Henry felt so strongly about American freedom from England that he once said "Give me liberty or give me death."

Celebrating the Past

Virginia is still an important part of our nation's government since it is so near the capital of the United States, Washington, D.C. Many government offices are located in Virginia today, but the Virginia of yesterday has not been forgotten. In fact, you can visit several places in Virginia to see how people lived and worked during Colonial times. The Jamestown settlement has been rebuilt and receives many visitors each year. In Colonial Williamsburg, pictured above, you can see how people lived in Virginia in the time of the Revolutionary War.

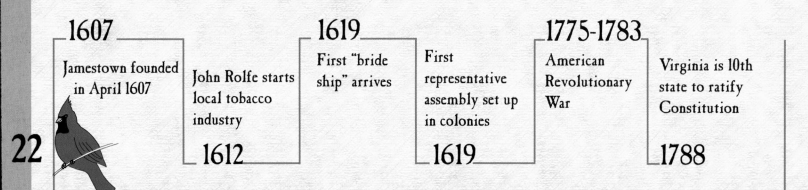

1607		1619		1775-1783	
Jamestown founded in April 1607	John Rolfe starts local tobacco industry	First "bride ship" arrives	First representative assembly set up in colonies	American Revolutionary War	Virginia is 10th state to ratify Constitution
	1612		1619		1788

Glossary

brutal (BRU-tul) Harsh, unfeeling, inhumane.

burgesses (BUR-jiss-iz) Citizens elected to help rule Colonial Virginia.

colonist (KAH-luh-nist) A person who lives in a colony.

colony (KAH-luh-nee) An area in a new country where a large group of people move, who are still ruled by the leaders and laws of their old country.

Declaration of Independence (deh-kluh-RAY-shun UV in-duh-PEN-dints) A paper signed on July 4, 1776, declaring that the American colonies were independent of Great Britain.

establish (uh-STA-blish) To found or set up.

export (ek-SPORT) To send something to another place to be sold.

governor (GUH-vuh-nur) An official that is put in charge of a colony by a king or queen.

indentured servant (in-DEN-churd SIR-vint) Person who has to work for another person for a fixed amount of time. In exchange, the master pays the servant's travel or living expenses.

independence (in-duh-PEN-dints) Not being ruled by another country.

investors (in-VES-turz) People who give money to pay for something (like a company) that they hope will bring them more money later on.

plantation (plan-TAY-shun) A very large farm where crops like tobacco and cotton were grown. Many plantation owners used slaves to work these farms.

rebel (ruh-BEL) To disobey the people or country in charge.

representative (rep-rih-ZEN-tuh-tiv) A person chosen to vote or speak for others.

revolutionary (REH-vuh-loo-shuh-nayr-ee) New way of doing or thinking about something.

united (yoo-NI-TID) To be joined or combined.

Index

Web Sites:

You can learn more about Colonial Virginia on the Internet.
Check out this Web site:

http://www.inmind.com/people/shammer/history.htm